FRAGMENTS OF COLLECTIVE MEMORY

ISBN: 9798875922374

DEDICATION

To the inhabitants of the tranquil village, whose intertwined stories weave the vibrant tapestry of collective memory. May this book be a testament to the past, a guide for the present, and an inspiration for the future.

TABLE OF CONTENTS

PREFACE

In this book, we delve into the depths of the collective memory of a tranquil village. Each chapter is a journey through the fragments that compose the rich tapestry of shared history. I invite the reader to explore forgotten corners and vivid memories that form the foundation of this narrative. May these words serve as a bridge between the past and the present, uniting us in the understanding that, even in the face of scars and challenges, resilience and solidarity can guide us to a more hopeful future.

ACKNOWLEDGMENTS

I extend my gratitude to all those whose stories and experiences contributed to the construction of this account. To the voices echoing in the pages of this book, I express my deep thanks. To the community that shaped this narrative, this work is dedicated to you.

PROLOGUE

As we enter each chapter, we are guided by characters whose lives intertwine with the fragments of collective memory. The once vibrant village, pulsating with promises and dreams, now faces the consequences of past choices. The narrative unfolds like a tapestry, revealing not only the light of the past but also the shadows that persist in the silent dance of history.

INTRODUCTION

In these pages, we witness the life of a village through the eyes of those who inhabit it. Each chapter reveals deeper layers of collective memory, from the first rays of sun awakening memories to the intricate web of solidarity that sustains the community. The story is like an incessant stream, flowing through time, reflecting the complexity of the human experience.

CHAPTER 1
FRAGMENTS OF COLLECTIVE MEMORY

In a tranquil village, the first rays of sun awaken intertwined memories of a bygone era. Maria, a wise elder, reflects on days when the community pulsed with vibrant energy, and hope clung to hearts like ivy on the walls of centennial houses. The main square was the epicenter of these memories, where children played under the shade of ancient trees, and smiles were exchanged like precious coins. Fragments of this collective memory begin to form around the promise of a new chapter, a chapter that began with a speech echoing through narrow streets.

The faces of neighbors, now weathered by time, were once young, filled with dreams. The leader's speech was like a symphony of possibilities, a promise of radiant days stretching ahead. Maria recalls how fragments of this promise came together to form a tapestry of expectations, with each thread representing a collective longing. However, as seasons passed, the fragments began to wear. The tapestry, once vivid, now showed signs of fading. The youth that gathered in the square now carried the weight of experiences they couldn't have anticipated. Childish laughter was replaced by sighs of a reality that proved more complex than the initial fragments suggested.

Citizens share stories of how the speech influenced their decisions. Some followed the guidance fervently, while others began to question the gaps between words and actions. Promises of prosperity and equality, once so clear, started to unravel amid unexpected challenges. The old church on the hill, once a silent witness to community celebrations, became a symbol of reflection. Maria recalls the congregation's murmurs, seeking answers to the changes shaping the village. The fragments are now like pieces of a scattered puzzle, waiting to be rearranged to reveal the hidden truth among their worn pieces. The last light of day paints the sky with shades of orange and purple, casting a shadow over the fragments that have now become scars in the village's history. Maria, with a mix of nostalgia and wisdom, concludes her collective memories, acknowledging that, even though the fragments have lost their original clarity, they continue to tell the story of a time when hope flourished and, for a brief moment, seemed infinite.

CHAPTER 2
REFLECTIONS IN THE STREAM

Along the stream winding through the village, reflections of collective memory come to life. The water that once mirrored radiant smiles and festive celebrations now reflects a landscape marked by changes. Children who once bathed in the fresh waters have grown, and their stories echo on the stream's banks like a gentle murmur.

The speech that permeated the atmosphere like a promising breeze left its mark on the landscape, and inhabitants find themselves confronted with the tangible results of decisions made decades ago. The promised prosperity shaped the village's architecture but also brought unforeseen challenges. Tall, modern buildings stand next to older structures, a visual collision between the past and present.

Along the stream's banks, itinerant vendors share their experiences, amidst laughter and sighs. Commerce, a vital part of the community, reflects the complexity of social and economic changes. Old markets now compete with shiny malls, and the traders' stories reveal the struggle to adapt to the demands of an ever-evolving world.

The continuously flowing water, witnessing the village's ups and downs, symbolizes the community's resilience. The fragments of collective memory, though dispersed, are like stones creating a path along the stream. Some are smooth and easy to tread, while others represent challenges overcome.

Older residents, sitting on benches by the stream, share stories of flourishing loves and deep disappointments. The speech that once inspired dreams of unity and understanding is now seen through the lens of experience, with nuances of both optimism and skepticism. The reflections in the stream, once so clear, now present distortions that tell the story not only of what was achieved but also of what was lost along the way.

As night falls, when the waters reflect the moonlight, the villagers continue to cast symbolic stones into the stream, adding silent chapters to their history. Collective memory, like the constant flow of the stream, remains uninterrupted, carrying with it the complexity of a community that persists, even in the face of time's marks.

CHAPTER 3
THE DANCE OF SHADOWS

As the sun sets over the village, the dance of shadows begins. In narrow alleys and beneath the ancient trees of the main square, shadows come to life, weaving stories of triumphs and tribulations. The architecture, once a symbol of progress, now casts shadows that echo the complexities of a changing society.

Maria, the wise elder, walks through the main square, where shadows of memories stretch across the cobblestone ground. She recalls the days when the square was a stage for communal celebrations, where laughter echoed like music. The shadows of those vibrant times now mingle with the present, creating a dance that reveals the intricate interplay between past and present.

The young generation, guided by the shadows of their ancestors, explores the square with a mix of curiosity and reverence. The elders, once the architects of the village's destiny, cast long shadows, a reminder of the legacy they carry. As the younger residents navigate the shadows, they find remnants of forgotten traditions and stories that shaped the community.

In the dance of shadows, Maria encounters the silhouette of a once-prominent leader whose speeches ignited the flames of hope. The leader's shadow, though diminished by time, still looms large over the square. Maria reflects on the promises made and the shadows cast by those promises. The village, once a canvas of aspirations, now bears the marks of choices that shaped its destiny.

The dance of shadows extends beyond the square, reaching every corner of the village. In the flickering light of lanterns, residents share stories of how the shadows influenced their lives. Some speak of the challenges they faced, while others celebrate the resilience that emerged from the shadows. The dance becomes a collective narrative, a reflection of the shared experiences that bind the community.

As the night deepens, the dance of shadows continues, casting a spell that connects generations. The village, illuminated by the moonlight, becomes a living testament to the dance of shadows—a dance that tells the story of a community shaped by the ebb and flow of time.

CHAPTER 4
TRACES OF THE PAST

In the quiet corners of the village, traces of the past linger like whispers carried by the wind. Dilapidated houses, weathered by time, stand as silent witnesses to the passage of generations. Maria, the wise elder, walks through these abandoned spaces, tracing the outlines of memories etched into the walls.

The remnants of once-bustling marketplaces tell stories of vibrant commerce and the exchange of goods. Maria recalls the laughter of children playing in the narrow streets, the aroma of street food wafting through the air, and the communal spirit that animated these spaces. Traces of the past, now faded, evoke a sense of nostalgia for a time when simplicity defined the rhythm of life.

In the remnants of an old library, Maria discovers dusty books and yellowed pages that hold the collective knowledge of the village. The library, once a sanctuary of wisdom, is now a forgotten relic. The fading ink on the pages narrates tales of bygone eras, capturing the intellectual pursuits that once thrived within the community.

The village cemetery, a sacred ground that echoes with the whispers of the departed, reveals the passage of time through weathered tombstones. Maria reads the names of ancestors who shaped the village's destiny and reflects on the significance of preserving their stories. Traces of the past, embodied in the cemetery's solemn atmosphere, become a bridge connecting the living to the departed.

As Maria walks through the ruins of an old school, memories of shared learning and youthful aspirations come to life. The blackboard, now covered in layers of dust, once bore the dreams and ambitions of the village's youth. Traces of the past, preserved in the decaying infrastructure, invite contemplation on the cyclical nature of life and the importance of passing on knowledge from one generation to the next.

The village, with its traces of the past, stands as a testament to the impermanence of human endeavors. In the quietude of these forgotten spaces, Maria recognizes the need to honor the legacy of the past while embracing the inevitability of change. Traces of the past, though fragile, carry the weight of history, guiding the present and shaping the future.

CHAPTER 5
SHADOWS OF NOSTALGIA

As dawn breaks, casting a gentle light over the village, shadows of nostalgia envelop the landscape. Maria, the wise elder, sits in the main square, where the echoes of bygone days resonate through the quiet morning air. The shadows of nostalgia, like a soft breeze, carry with them the fragrance of memories long cherished.

In the heart of the square, Maria recalls the gatherings that once filled the air with the scent of fresh flowers and homemade treats. The communal spirit, embodied in shared laughter and conversations, was the essence of the village's identity. Shadows of nostalgia bring forth images of festive celebrations, where the simple joys of life took center stage.

The village bakery, a cornerstone of community life, emerges in Maria's memories. The aroma of freshly baked bread and the warmth of the ovens created a comforting ambiance. Residents, young and old, would gather to savor the delights and share stories. The bakery, now a mere shell of its former self, stands as a silent witness to the passage of time.

The main square, once adorned with vibrant decorations during festivals, now bears the marks of weathering and neglect. Maria reflects on the changes that have shaped the square's identity and the shadows of nostalgia that cling to its every corner. The memories of joyous dances and lively music resonate through the quietude, reminding the village of its vibrant past.

In the shadows of nostalgia, Maria encounters the spirits of departed loved ones who once filled the square with their presence. The interconnectedness of generations becomes palpable as memories intertwine, creating a tapestry that transcends time. The village, bathed in the soft glow of morning light, becomes a canvas painted with shadows of nostalgia—a canvas that tells the story of a community shaped by the beauty of fleeting moments.

As Maria watches the sunrise, she acknowledges the bittersweet nature of nostalgia. The shadows cast by memories, though tinged with longing, carry the warmth of shared experiences. In the embrace of nostalgia, the village finds solace and a renewed appreciation for the richness of its history.

CHAPTER 6
TRACES OF RESISTANCE

As we explore the traces of resistance, we encounter intertwined narratives of courage and perseverance. Records of peaceful demonstrations, clandestine pamphlets, and resilient street art echo the determination of a community that refused to be silenced. The remnants of these acts of resistance, now faded by time, tell the story of a people who challenged adversity in the pursuit of justice and freedom.

In a central square, the monument erected in honor of those who protested becomes a beacon of inspiration. The words carved in stone recount the saga of ordinary individuals who became reluctant heroes, facing repression with courage and conviction. The community, as they touch these stones weathered by wind and time, connects with the strength that sprouted from the grassroots of society.

Traces of resistance also manifest in stories passed down from generation to generation. Around campfires, elders share tales of battles fought not only with weapons but with the resilience of the human spirit. The lessons learned in these narratives fuel the flame of determination, inspiring future generations to embrace the responsibility of shaping their own destiny.

Unveiling these traces, the community confronts the complexity of the struggle for justice and equality. Each mark on the fabric of time tells a story of resistance that transcends the individual, evolving into a collective legacy of courage and perseverance. The journey reveals that even in the shadows of adversity, the light of resistance continues to shine, guiding the way to a future shaped by the relentless pursuit of truth and freedom.

CHAPTER 7
INVISIBLE SCARS

Invisible scars tell a story of pain and trauma, a narrative unrecorded in books but deeply engraved in the souls of those who faced challenging times. In these fragments of collective memory, we discover the emotional heritage of a community that carries the weight of its history.

Silently, invisible scars reveal the agony of lives shattered by oppressive systems. They bear witness to sleepless nights, stifled sighs, and dreams interrupted by cruel realities. These scars transcend the physical, delving into the depths of the psyche, where pain transforms into resilience, and resilience becomes a form of resistance.

Exploring these scars, we uncover the complexity of human interactions under the weight of policies that neglected collective well-being. Those who carry these invisible marks become reluctant guardians of memory, reminding us that the true extent of the struggle goes beyond what the eyes can see.

In daily interactions, these scars shape perspectives and influence decisions. Sometimes, they silently guide the hand of those writing laws, inspiring changes that transcend the bounds of time. Invisible scars, often overlooked, are silent witnesses to human resilience and the ability to transform pain into strength.

As we delve into these stories, we are confronted with the question: how can we heal invisible scars? Perhaps the answer lies in the collective acceptance of our shared history, in understanding that acknowledging pain is the first step toward healing.

CHAPTER 8
THE WEB OF SOLIDARITY

The web of solidarity, woven with threads of shared experiences, reveals itself as an antidote to invisible scars. In this chapter, we explore the human connections that emerge from adversity, forming a support network that sustains the community.

Faced with collective challenges, people come together, creating an intricate web of solidarity. This web knows no boundaries, uniting hearts and minds in a common purpose: overcoming adversity. It transcends superficial differences and highlights the shared essence of the human experience.

Solidarity often manifests in simple yet powerful ways. It can be a friendly gesture, an encouraging word, or the simple act of being present in difficult moments. Enveloped in the web of solidarity, we realize that healing invisible scars begins with genuine connections between people.

In the intertwining of these threads, we discover stories of compassion and empathy that transcend the limits of time. The web of solidarity not only heals individually but also strengthens the social fabric, creating a solid foundation for collective rebirth.

As we explore the fragments of collective memory, we are reminded that even in the darkest pages of history, the light of solidarity can illuminate the path to a more hopeful future.

CHAPTER 9

RISE FROM THE ASHES

Rising from the ashes, the community finds its collective strength to rebuild what was lost. In this chapter, we examine the moments when resilience becomes a bright flame, dissipating the darkness that hung over people's lives.

Desolation often triggers an unexpected rebirth. As people face adversity, they discover an inner courage that was dormant. This awakening is the seed of resurrection, a promise of new beginnings even in the most challenging circumstances.

Resurrection is not just an individual act; it is a collective phenomenon. Entire communities can emerge from the ashes, guided by the determination to build something better. This process of renewal reveals the incredible human ability to transform pain into opportunity, sadness into inspiration.

Each story of resurgence is unique, but all share a common thread of hope. As the ashes disperse, new horizons emerge, offering a glimpse of a future born from resilience and solidarity.

Exploring these accounts of rebirth, we are reminded that even in the darkest moments, the human capacity to rise is an indomitable force. The journey from ashes to resurrection invites us to believe in the promise of a brighter tomorrow, shaped by the lessons learned in the challenging pages of the past.

CHAPTER 10
THE TAPESTRY OF MEMORY

Concluding our journey through the fragments of collective memory, we enter the final chapter, where the diverse threads of experience intertwine to create a unique and intricate tapestry. Here, we seek to understand how individual stories connect to form the rich weave of collective memory.

Each account, each shared memory, contributes to the weaving of this tapestry. Singular experiences, whether of joy, sorrow, triumph, or loss, meld to create a broader portrait of the community. It is in the union of these elements that the true essence of collective memory is revealed.

The tapestry of memory is dynamic and ever-evolving. New events and narratives are continually interwoven, altering the composition of the image that represents the shared history of a community. The diversity of colors and textures reflects the inherent complexity of the human experience.

As we explore these final fragments, we are led to reflect on the fluid nature of memory. It is not static but a living organism that adapts and transforms over time. This chapter concludes our exploration, leaving us with the understanding that collective memory is a work in progress, always open to new chapters and interpretations.